César Franck

SONATA IN A MAJOR

for FLUTE and PIANO

Edited by

JAMES GALWAY

Piano part edited by Phillip Moll

GREAT PERFORMER'S EDITION

ED 3797
ISBN 978-0-7935-9809-0

G. SCHIRMER, Inc.

DISTRIBUTED BY

7777 W. BLUEMOUND RD. P.O. BOX 13819 MILWAUKEE, WI 53213

JAMES GALWAY

James Galway is one of today's best-known performers, a rare example of the musician who is equally successful in both classical and popular repertoire. Since he left the Berlin Philharmonic Orchestra in 1975, he has appeared regularly on the world's stages and television screens playing works that range from Mozart, Bach and Vivaldi through Debussy, Poulenc and Khachaturian to Japanese and Irish melodies, Country, Pop and Jazz.

Born in Belfast, Northern Ireland, James Galway decided at the age of 14 to make the flute his career, and soon scholarships enabled him to study in London, later in Paris, and then with the celebrated Marcel Moyse. Returning to England, he took a variety of orchestral jobs that eventually led to his being appointed principal flutist with the London Symphony Orchestra and, in 1969, the Berlin Philharmonic Orchestra under Herbert Von Karajan.

After six years there Mr. Galway felt it was time to establish himself as a solo artist. With his extraordinary virtuosity and charisma it did not take long — within a year he had recorded four albums for RCA Records, given 120 concerts and appeared as soloist with the four major London orchestras. Since then he has circled the globe several times with a varied schedule of recitals, concertos, chamber music and masterclasses.

In addition to performing, Mr. Galway devotes himself to enlarging the repertoire for his instrument, transcribing works and commissioning new ones.

SONATA

1

Piano part edited by Phillip Moll

CÉSAR FRANCK
Edited by James Galway

2

3
RECITATIVO-FANTASIA

26

4